SEASCAPE: NEEDLE'S EYE

Seascape: Needle's Eye

GEORGE OPPEN

THE SUMAC PRESS

Fremont, Michigan

for Linda

Table of Contents

From A Phrase Of Simone Weil's And Some Words Of Hegel's

In   back   deep the jewel
The treasure
No   Liquid
Pride of the living life's liquid
Pride in the sandspit wind this ether this other this element all
It is I or I believe
We are the beaks of the ragged birds
Tune of the ragged bird's beaks
In the tune of the winds
Ob via   the obvious
Like a fire of straws
Aflame in the world or else poor people hide
Yourselves together   Place
Place where   desire
Lust of the eyes the pride of life and foremost of the storm's
Multitude moves the wave belly-lovely
Glass of the glass sea shadow of water
On the open water no other way
To come here the outer
Limit of the ego

The Occurrences

Limited air   drafts
In the treasure house moving and the movements of the living
Things fall   something balanced   Move
With all one's force
Into the commonplace that pierces or erodes

The mind's structure but nothing
Incredible happens
It will have happened to that other
The survivor   The survivor
To him it happened

Rooted in basalt
Night hums like the telephone dial tone blue gauze
Of the forge flames the pulse
Of infant
Sorrows at the crux

Of the timbers
When the middle Kingdom
Warred with beasts Middle Things the elves the

Magic people in their world
Among the plant roots   hopes
Which are the hopes
Of small self interest called

Superstition chitinous
Toys of the children wings
Of the wasp

Animula

animula blandula vagula

Chance and chance and thereby starlit
All that was to be thought
Yes
Comes down the road   Air of the waterfronts   black air

Over the iron bollard   the doors cracked

In the starlight things the things continue
Narrative   their long instruction and the tide running
Strong as a tug's wake   shorelights'

Fractured dances across rough water a music
Who would believe it
Not quite one's own
With one always   the black verse   the turn and the turn

At the lens' focus   the crystal pool   innavigable

Torrent torment Eden's
Flooded valley   dramas

Of dredged waters
A wind blowing out

11

And out to sea   the late the salt times cling

In panicked
Spirals at the hull's side sea's streaks floating
Curved on the sea little pleasant soul wandering

Frightened

The small mid-ocean
Moon lights the winches

West

Elephant, say, scraping its dry sides
In a narrow place as he passes says yes

This is true

So one knows?   and the ferns unfurling   leaves

In the wind

. . . sea   from which . .

'We address the future?   '

Unsure of the times
Unsure I can answer

To myself   We have been ignited
Blazing

In wrath we await

The rare poetic
Of veracity that huge art whose geometric
Light seems not its own in that most dense world West and East
Have denied have hated have wandered in   *precariousness*

Like a new fire

Will burn out the roots
One thinks of steep fields
Of brown grass
In the mountains it seems they lie
Aslant in the thin
Burning air and among clouds the sun
Passes boulders   grass blades   sky clad things

In nakedness
Inseperable   *the children will say*

Our parents waited in the woods   precarious

Transparent as the childhood of the world
Growing old   the seagulls sound like the voices of children
          wilder than children wildest of children the waves'
          riot
Brilliant as the world
Up side down   Not obstinate islands

This is the seaboard   New skilled fishermen
In the great bays and the narrow bights

Of Hours

' . . . as if a nail whose wide head
were time and space . . '

at the nail's point the hammer - blow
undiminished

Holes   pitfalls open
In the cop's accoutrement

Crevasse

The destitute metal

Jail metal

Impoverished   Intimate
As a Father did you know that

Old friend   old poet
Tho you'd walked

Familiar streets
And glittered with change the circle

Destroyed its content
Persists   the common

Place   image
The initial light   Walk on the walls

The walls of the fortress   the countryside
Broad in the night light the sap rises

Out of obscurities the sap rises
The sap not exhausted   Movement
Of the stone   Music
Of the tenement

Also is this lonely theme   Earth
My sister

Lonely sister my sister but why did I weep
Meeting that poet again what was that rage

Before Leger's art poster
In war time Paris perhaps art

Is one's mother and father   O rage
Of the exile   Fought ice

Fought shifting stones
Beyond the battlement

Crevasse   Fought

No man
But the fragments of metal
Tho there were men there were men   Fought
No man but the fragments of metal
Burying my dogtag with H
For Hebrew in the rubble of Alsace

I must get out of here

Father   he thinks   *father*

Disgrace of dying

Old friend   old poet
If you did not look

What is it you 'loved'
Twisting your voice   your walk

Wet roads

Hot sun on the hills

He walks twig-strewn streets
Of the rain

Walks homeward

Unteachable

Song, The Winds Of Downhill

'out of poverty
to begin

again'   impoverished

of tone of pose that common
wealth

of parlance   Who
so poor the words

would   with   and   take on substantial

meaning   handholds   footholds

to dig in one's heels   sliding

hands and heels beyond the residential
lots   the plots   it is a poem

which may be sung
may well be sung

Some San Francisco Poems

1

*Moving over the hills, crossing the irrigation
canals perfect and profuse in the mountains the
streams of women and men walking under the high-
tension wires over the brown hills*

*in the multiple world of the fly's
multiple eye the songs they go to hear on
this occasion are no one's own*

*Needle's eye   needle's eye   but in the ravine
again and again on the massive spike the song
clangs*

*as the tremendous volume of the music takes
over obscured by their long hair they seem
to be mourning*

2

A Morality Play : Preface

Lying full length
On the bed in the white room

Turns her eyes to me

Again,

Naked . .

Never to forget her naked eyes

Beautiful and brave
Her naked eyes

Turn inward

Feminine light

The unimagined
Feminine light

Feminine ardor

Pierced and touched

Tho all say
Huddled among each other

'Love'

The play begins with the world

A city street
Leads to the bay

Tamalpais in cloud

Mist over farmlands

Local knowledge
In the heavy hills

The great loose waves move landward
Heavysided in the wind

Grass and trees bent
Along the length of coast in the continual wind

The ocean pounds in her mind
Not the harbor leading inward
To the back bay and the slow river
Recalling flimsy Western ranches
The beautiful hills shine outward

Sunrise   the raw fierce fire
Coming up past the sharp edge

And the hoof marks on the mountain

Shines in the white room

Provincial city
Not alien enough

To naked eyes

This city died young

You too will be shown this

You will see the young couples

Leaving again in rags

3

So with artists.   How pleasurable
to imagine that, if only they gave
up their art, the children would be
healed,   would live.

Irving Younger in *The Nation*

'And Their Winter And Night In Disguise'

The sea and a crescent strip of beach
Show between the service station and a deserted shack

A creek drains thru the beach
Forming a ditch
There is a discarded super-market cart in the ditch
That beach is the edge of a nation

There is something like shouting along the highway
A California shouting
On the long fast highway over the California mountains

Point Pedro
Its distant life

It is impossible the world should be either good or bad
If its colors are beautiful or if they are not beautiful
If parts of it taste good or if no parts of it taste good
It is as remarkable in one case as the other
                                        As against this

We have suffered fear, we know something of fear
And of humiliation mounting to horror

The world above the edge of the foxhole belongs to the
    flying bullets, leaden superbeings
For the men grovelling in the foxhole danger, danger in
    being drawn to them

These little dumps
The poem is about them

Our hearts are twisted
In dead men's pride

Dead men crowd us
Lean over us

In the emplacements

The skull spins
Empty of subject

The hollow ego

Flinching from the war's huge air

Tho we are delivery boys and bartenders

We will choke on each other

Minds may crack

But not for what is discovered

Unless that everyone knew
And kept silent

Our minds are split
To seek the danger out

From among the miserable soldiers

4

Anniversary Poem

'the picturesque
common lot'   the unwarranted light

Where everyone has been

The very ground of the path
And the litter grow ancient

A shovel's scratched edge
So like any other man's

We are troubled by incredulity
We are troubled by scratched things

Becoming familiar
Becoming extreme

Let grief
Be
So it be ours

Nor hide one's eyes
As tides drop along the beaches in the thin wash of
        breakers

And so desert each other

--lest there be nothing

                    the Indian girl walking across the desert, the
sunfish under the boat

How shall we say how this happened, these stories, our
                stories

Scope, mere size, a kind of redemption

Exposed still and jagged on the San Francisco hills

Time and depth before us, paradise of the real, we
            know what it is

To find now depth, not time, since we cannot, but depth

To come out safe,   to end well

We have begun to say good bye
To each other
And cannot say it

5

The Translucent Mechanics

Combed thru the piers the wind
Moves in the clever city
Not in the doors but the hinges
Finds the secret of motion
As tho the hollow ships moved in their voices,   murmurs
Flaws
In the wind
Fear   fear
At the lumber mastheads
And fetched a message out of the sea again

Say angel   say powers

Obscurely   'things
And the self'

Prosody

Sings

In the stones

        to entrust
To a poetry of statement

At close quarters

A living mind
'and that one's own'

             what then   what spirit

Of the bent seas

                    Archangel

of the tide
brimming

in the moon-streak

                    comes in whose absence
earth crumbles

6

Silver as
The needle's eye

Of the horizon in the noise
Of their entrance row on row the waves
Move landward   conviction's

Net of branches
In the horde of events the sacred swarm avalanche
Masked in the sunset

Needle after needle more numerous than planets

Or the liquid waves
In the tide rips

We believe   we believe

Beyond the cable car streets
And the picture window

Lives the glittering crumbling night
Of obstructions and the stark structures

That carry wires over the mountain
One writes in the presence of something
Moving close to fear
I dare pity no one
Let the rafters pity
The air in the room
Under the rafters
Pity
In the continual sound
Are chords
Not yet struck
Which will be struck
Nevertheless yes

7

O withering seas
Of the doorstep and local winds unveil

The face of art

Carpenter, plunge and drip in the sea   Art's face
We know that face

More blinding than the sea   a haunted house   a limited

Consensus unwinding

Its powers
Toward the thread's end

In the record of great blows   shocks
Ravishment   devastation   the wood splintered

The keyboard gone in the rank grass swept her hand
Over the strings and the thing rang out

Over the rocks and the ocean
Not my poem   Mr Steinway's

Poem   Not mine   A 'marvelous' object
Is not the marvel of things

        twisting the new
Mouth   forcing the new
Tongue   But it rang

8

The Taste

Old ships are preserved
For their queer silence of obedient seas
Their cutwaters floating in the still water
With their cozy black iron work
And Swedish seamen dead   the cabins
Hold the spaces of their deaths
And the hammered nails of necessity
Carried thru the oceans
Where the moon rises grandly
In the grandeur of cause
We have a taste for bedrock
Beneath this spectacle
To gawk at
Something is wrong with the antiques, a black fluid
Has covered them, a black splintering
Under the eyes of young wives
People talk wildly, we are beginning to talk wildly, the wind
At every summit
Our overcoats trip us
Running for the bus
Our arms stretched out
In a wind from what were sand dunes

9

The Impossible Poem

Climbing the peak of Tamalpais the loose
Gravel underfoot

And the city shining with the tremendous wrinkles
In the hills and the winding of the bay
Behind it, it faces the bent ocean

Streetcars
Rocked thru the city and the winds
Combed their clumsy sides

In clumsy times

Sierras withering
Behind the storefronts

And sanity the roadside weed
Dreams of sports and sportsmanship

In the lucid towns paralyzed
Under the truck tires
Shall we relinquish

Sanity to redeem
Fragments and fragmentary
Histories in the towns and the temperate streets
Too shallow still to drown in or to mourn
The courageous and precarious children

10

But So As By Fire

The darkness of trees
Guards this life
Of the thin ground
That covers the rock ledge

Among the lanes and magic
Of the Eastern woods

The beauty of silence
And broken boughs

And the homes of small animals

The green leaves
Of young plants
Above the dark green moss
In the sweet smell of rot

The pools and the trickle of freshwater

First life,   rotting life
Hidden starry life it is not yet

A mirror
Like our lives

We have gone
As far as is possible

Whose lives reflect light
Like mirrors

One had not thought
To be afraid

Not of shadow but of light

Summon one's powers

Exodus

Miracle of the children   the brilliant
Children   the word
Liquid as woodlands   Children?

When she was a child I read Exodus
To my daughter   'The children of Israel . . . '

Pillar of fire
Pillar of cloud

We stared at the end
Into each other's eyes   Where
She said hushed

Were the adults   We dreamed to each other
Miracle of the children
The brilliant children   Miracle

Of their brilliance   Miracle
of